How Rain Records Its Alphabet

HOW RAIN
RECORDS
ITS ALPHABET

John Tritica

La Alameda Press • Albuquerque

Thanks to the editors of the following magazines
where some of these poems first appeared:
*BullHead; Central Park; disturbed guillotine;
First Intensity; House Organ; lower limit speech;
Nexus; no røses review; Panoply; Printed Matter* (Japan);
Solo; Take Five; and *Talisman.*

Katherine Kuehn, artist/publisher of Salient Seedling Press,
created a one-of-a-kind broadside of
"Not Masterpieces, Planting Astonishments".

I wish also to express gratitude to the following group of writer-friends
who have read these poems in their original form. Gene Frumkin, Mary
Rising Higgins, Kathleen Linnell, Niklas Törnlund, Sheila E. Murphy,
David Abel, Dan Giancola, Joe Napora, Sharon di Maria, Stephen Ellis,
and Phyllis Hoge—your critique has helped immensely.

Copyright 1998 © by John Tritica

Cover painting: "Wet Brush #7"
ink on paper • J.B. Bryan

ISBN: 1-888809-09-4
Library of Congress Number: 98-067348

La Alameda Press
9636 Guadalupe Trail NW
Albuquerque, New Mexico 87114

for
Lucas and Natalia Tritica,
Karen Fischer,
& Joe Napora

Contents

Haven: an introduction

Gardens and gardening, object and action, image and the telling how it grows out of itself—the development of a *cogito's* momentum and realization—all are determining contraries which, like a good pair of hands, combine in John Tritica's work to provide the base-line for improvisations through which timings of both person as perceiver and objects *as perceived* are drawn into brevities of recognition that lead always to a present grounded in the factual, yet presented *as an activity* through which the world as made and made again remains singular. Complete, yet equally provisional. *Mortal.* Open to change in the sense that a jazz improvisation is thought to "run changes" on a theme, renewing it, as in "Star Garden", by discovering the interlocking of incidentals that yield essentiality: "The Big Dipper splits / juniper scent engages // the skylight's / notes. You in- // volve a weed / blade to open // yet another glyph." *As if* opening out is what one thus were enclosed by. Tritica's art in this is the sharp one of discriminating the con(tra)-textual in which use = paradise.

The relationship between gardens and paradise is an old one. Garden as yard goes back to an Indo-European root **gerdh-*, meaning *to enclose*, and further **gher-*, *to grasp*, while paradise derives from an Avestani (old Iranian) root *pairi-daeza*, a combination of *around* and *wall*. This ability to enclose and grasp has primarily to do with the dual sense of a focusing and a making, especially as these relate the body and its perceptual organs through the *cogito* made clear in language to how this continuum may be applied to natural form, which is thus "enclosed"—grasped—as a measured sequence, very much the Blakean equation that orders the natural or "wild" triadic foundation *stone, forest, beast*, through its intelligences, the *head, heart and bowels* in order to achieve the correlative and useful *city, garden and flock*.

Robert Duncan, in his 1965 Berkeley lecture "Psyche, Myth, and the Moment of Truth," makes a point about "scale" in terms of what he called "the ill-kept garden"—i.e., an *inclusive*, "weedy" one—suggesting that the "obsessive wildness" of this "keeps itself"—tends itself—and that our representation of it, in all the austere and lawful formalities that language itself, and our use of it, requires, is evident also in the growth of this very garden, or more literally *field*, which Duncan then goes on to correlate with the universe, the wonder of which is literally *what it contains*, not that it is at all *important: Form* as instant, such that one moves with where one recognizes it.

So with Tritica. *Locale* is as essential to his practice as *location*, though not in the sense of Olson's Gloucester; in Tritica's practice, locale and location act dually as an intense focusing device through which to discover timings that lead to the formal extension of discovery in ways similar to the body's active extension within its environment. His emphasis is on *use*, its realization and purpose, the practicum of *measure*. The improvising dialectic so evident here dovetails perception and mind to provide an index by which temporal location, movement, and the elliptical intercession of "seeing what one inherently knows" as the form thus made, is given residence in no hierarchy but change and the perpetuum of transformation—yet without also sacrificing the more delicate sensual aspect of "being there".

And there's your "haven"—the heaven of enclosure—in the opening *out* of language to its referent as equally *sounding* and *text* that, together, comprise a "grasping" of location simultaneous to a music-footed accompaniment of one's passing and earnest focus that carries one through one's elemental consciousness fulfilled by an ability to *name*. In a word, the work *feels* true as both narrative and image continue formally to unfold. Here, there is movement, rhythm, the heart's beats, days passage, a season's heat caught in the immediate screech of a jay—all and any each of which, together, comprise the *sincere*. "Motion, Pattern, Aroma" lays "the program" (if you will) clearly out—"All morning following scales through / the bare elm // So what times I discover / crowns the leaves reticulations // And proves what's random. // Frees gardening in how time sets me / in motion, pattern, aroma. // When I talk stages, blanks, / tables, spirals. // Cite what tries to hide." The use of language as provisional method toward location moved through its passing realizations is equally the *cogito* of a "digging in" and this dialectical progression of both *moving out* and *staying put* makes Tritica's both a sensual and radical—i.e., *essential*—art that each of us might usefully practice.

Stephen Ellis
06.01.98

The Tune of Chance

Track a holographic grid and
organize the particles to eagle
maze (dis)closure. Not there,
virtually there. Sidewalks,

paper cuts, precise mirror
to reflect slim lines,
branches to scrape flesh.

The corner's a tuck and fold,
knot a daring procedure, this.
If the axis tilts my alphabet
views invent a common wealth.

The razor's a fractal, limits
patterns, designs us.
Settle for entering a wind tunnel.

What you drive, curved space.

You interview slates, choreograph
elastic punctuation: a wild solo
tense over saxes, locates
the nexus of released shrieks.

Synthetic automation can't
contain the drums' ambition.

A knot beat hardware slides
aloof stares, margins.

You shift from the Möbius strip to
tangled ribbons, bits of chance,
dialogues in quaking.

Now you turn to ventriloquism,
now to commas and meteors.

Sudden Tracings

As if winter came in a day
to lose drift, tunnels rip

the arroyo maintains its weight
shifting pressures in diurnal chill.

Direction of sunlight
lengthens shadowweed.

A conversation among needles
descends the windjets

deftly, juniper smoke.
Neural relays, hearing shares

discrete bits, proceedings.
Branches smolder a cirrus sky

tight against the skin.
One warms his hands.

One somersaults in snow.
One lights the end of a stick.

The twirl patterned signatures
a slow shutter take out

frozen dusk in frames.
Where sudden seasons turn

a spark around extended hands.

Unwobbling Pivot

for Karen and for Will

   Wind rills shout.
Not clatter   shoots of stone
      the blows back.

To circumscribe the crystalline
rays brim on the Strait mirror.

Steadiness waves in torrents
haze bands
         across Washington shores.

Clouds cumulate in Olympic glaciers.

The hand grows autonomous. Rocks
float in the Strait. Barnacles
      fan out the currents' frame.

Streams feed mouths   firs
      temple hemlocks

tier delights
            gull glide
sitting in unwobbling pivot

rush tide   shivers goose arms.

Wade to knees   too chilled
for plunge. Sand clarifies
the sounds   coves
                an echo
        stirs glaciers
    reverberations

not too distant

Birdwoman Improvisation Beginning with Lines by Nathanial Tarn

as if she were making a book
for birds to read

she gathers drift cypress
plover down, pine branches

to feather her arms
and kelp the shore

to stretch the Pacific
surf the long strand

what becomes the naked hands
the legs kicking air circles

in each droplet she presses
sand into presence

and her statues print
gold shadows

"she who weaves"
"she who returns"

the gaze barbs
keen minds

that the play
of wings

Retrieval

Horizon hazes Pt. Dune's crags.
Try to edge flatness
the swells' undulations.

Solidity specifies
the sand drift.
A plover locates sand crabs
shadows the tide.

A sip of coffee. Gull down
squawks, a wave grain shifts.

In case of hunger, turn
the wind's motion. Oblique
categories s(t)imulate waves.

Haze ports appear from
non-static points.
Found bottlecap in
a gull's beak.

Casts a line off the pier
as if to infuse the ocean's
electricity. A quarter

in the telescope
brings taut sails.

Talking at the same time.
I try to move away

from my métier. Not the
usual winter breakers.

The gravity of the fishers.
Vapor jet trails, cirrus
streaks at the lines.

How many have you caught?
I roll on the strand
anticipate the rain.

To score air completion
winter rays its son
time for retrieval.

Climate Control

for Bruce Cockburn

Publish skin.

Strange train ride,
cornered by chain saws.

Travelling in tandem,
oxen yoke drives.

Catch the clod.

Etherized against the retina.
Chinese gardener, jade pond. If
the forest falls, publish brain damage

from Malaysia to Brazil.

Do we oxygenate the years? Coves.
Macaw dust, dry plummage. Orchestrate
the verb's slash and burn.

Publish sugar.

Coffee gets you going on end.
All mahagony, that table. You nationalize
for geographic returns. Food for clash. Echo,
if we fall.

Was no tree there?

How to prove our arms to them? Rain.
A blight gets to the trunk first. Decide age
by inventing the rings. Secretary birds the spoils.

Agrimachine.

Oxygen driven on teak wheels. Dog bark withers,
greening the house. If we are not forest,
our breath cannot buy.

Point Lobos Improvisation Beginning with a Line by e.e. cummings

whose texture compels me
with the colour of its countries

the cypresses at Point Lobos recall
van Gogh's explosion

your eyes incandesce beyond
the language we persuade

another revolution in our quills
our daily handsprings

the whales rise and spout
draw us on

their vaulted melodies
we swim with phytoplankton

crash in tidal pools
in and out of anemones

resting in your fingers
a balm, a pressure

a moist drowsiness
our capacity sustains

the sand's provinces
lattices of salt crystals

one to the other
we turn toward exhaustion

lick hunger from our thighs
on a bed of bronze play

The Knowing

for Roger Daniels

Afternoon
Sunday light
through streaked glass
between mullions
what hovers, reaches
the outstretched hand.

Cirrus feathers
cottonwood
what alights
articulates
Satie's flourish.

Shadowplays
over your shoulder
always late
afternoon performs

to set out, capture rays,
the filter
that would extend
remains open.

"Gnossiennes" would
digest what fire?
Is it a desert of words
or cataract of notes

in Satie's lines?
Lent. Tentative.
Circle around the room.

Questionez. As if
the first day
were perpetual
small gestures.
Finger pad notes
light emphasis
the flickers.

One moment only
tres luissant
the house to lose
its roof.

Munissez-vous de clairvoyance.
Satie shifts
not just furniture
the walls themselves
shade the blue
steady entropy.

A child opens each petal
of a rose
knowing you perform
the indispensable.

We depart
questioning

high desert, dusklight
elements
finger nimbly.

To find time opens
the pace, Middle-Eastern,
common phrasing
to be lost.

Dahlias through the blinds.
Satie addresses
the burgundy, the shine
in each flower.
Pollen gathers
a durable repast,
the palette's bouquet.
The way your shoulders
remain utterly still.

Around the Equinox

Tithonia's orange bursts
  green time, stable.
Shadow of arm hair
  elongation of thumb
   appreciates
      light degree.
Pineapple sage, Mexican sage, violet dahlias.

  Night rain saturates
   spinach seeds, waiting
    for release.

   Slight membrane, eye true tolerance
   the rainshade swells.
      Velocity visits the air.
       Hail-shredded canna leaves
       like strange plummage, you say.

   Light concedes the dusk
      sooner
         than what's electric.
   When space is small
      every gesture lands
         around a seasonal pivot
   by virtue of residence.

   To give in to cold bare feet
      pine cricket

sprinkler on creeping thyme.

Urgency in the periphery.
Not only insect wings
in the night

outlines of the apricot tree.

To wait for green delivery
on the last page, a different ink.
For earlier morning light, the sound
of hummingbirds.

Autumn meridians, lightpaths, migrations.

To follow the globe's tilt
is to land time's alternate
tuning.

What Remains

Late autumn quickens
shadows, each tone notes

birdsong punctuates
what ensemble provides:

dry broomgrass, garlic chives,
grapevines, cannas, sunflowers.

Skinlight intelligence, supple flesh,
the shoulder that extends reach.

But plot the sunlight's tilt
only to find it implodes

to a mathematics not within hand
to cease time deliberations.

It's still the way chimes
note what remains of the wind.

To turnaround motion, autumn
remembers how the eye

is altered, acuity rushing ahead.

Cold Lines

How to study the work
when fermenting processes
occur, or navigate
the crash course in chaos.

To maintain when the cold wind
blows through the door
the moon long since visible.

As the mix draws light
time careens through
arteries of escape.

But to hold in sync moments
of precise cold location
palpable models or resolutions.
To collude with what's invisible

tap it out
in reasonable time, touch,
brush, sight, paint.

Sunflowers still there, sudden freeze,
dead against the horizon.
She flips on the outside light
certain cold will
shove me inside. The desire

to shape it close, not narrow
or admit various forms
of debris as part, not pattern.

To let chill urgency provide
direction. Not to have noticed
the hummingbird feeder remains.

Till sight's torn freely
tithonia stalks, burnt umber.
Cold glass tabletop
shapes what must please
reflects a light feast.

Now the locust tree, now
the cherry, gestures wind
sound calliope. Dusk lines,
sky bleeds, the moon
plies bare chemistry.

Legends

(Map of the Human Heart)

Everywhere I go I'm bad luck.
The map lines lead in an arctic swirl
the white world freezes chaos.

Enduring my own autonomy, the sea is a circle.
The maps tell all, this life that I don't choose.
Disease mocks stability.

To understand the body's longitude,
the latitude's range.
In painting, to breach winter's pallor.

My view of the crow upside down.
I don't know this tree,
but that I have to reach anything leafy.

We're going to take a look inside you.
Surveying disaster, I find my own state.
When the ship departs, whales spout.
Ice blind crystals, bombing's fury.

Where oil burns the equivocal torch
mine blazes for a *half-breed girl.*
Coughing blood on the snow:
You haven't been in a war, I have.
Which affiliation did I leave
when deceit reached me?

To join because someone told me not to.
I crumple the leaf for white man's business.
She wakes me with mirror-glare newness.
Time scream delays, my aerial light connections.

If my photos ring the right aircraft
we meet in music and danger.
The plaster smokes in our hair,
your stocking on the tympani.

Surprise arrives the cinematic sweep.
Whether heart or mind, I locate the current
in light's extreme.

Would you rend what failed luck promises?
Best of both worlds in bitter whiskey.
Sometimes all they tell you is you're lost.

I struggle with ice:
the maps tell only where I could be.

Approaching the Equinox

In different shades of blue ink.
The chimes set pace tone
afternoon syncopation
following shapely contours,

colors, sound that enthralls
meshed cognition, tentative,
affective, not to maintain
defenses, but to slip through
times, what shape equals, words

we use toward twilight.
Gives way to the string of lights
never taken down, in its own image
coreopsis already pushing through
the soil. How to sort it out?

A sip of coffee, form's challenge
fades to the foreground.
An opium poppy in chinks of walkway.
To warrant semantic excess
but to define or extend
beyond the bleachers.

Wine spot on the page.
If I could sever bare grapevines
will soon need pruning. Sundown
caught in pecan branches.

When the equinox arrives
I'm not in shorts.
Take no false neologisms
or pregnancy might result.
To return to the circular
is to reroute the straight line.
Allow to wing graphic sport
the idea's no conclusion.

If you want a poem
find a blank page.

Spread out aural portraits.
On the island, suddenly
a longing for the desert.
Legs and hands now chilled.
Glass table-top with an orange.

Reading poetry is to write the world.

To explore this in the extraordinary
everyday. What gains? What loses?
Is infused into various readings
and corporeal movements belonging together.
Yet to maintain energy and attention
at the periphery, or scope where
possibility's actual. Still the feet and legs cold.

Where is the room inside poetry?
Or corridors, where we would

approach opposite horizons. As sleep takes me
the dendrites operate beyond their stated design.

Fragility stalks nerve endings.
Always the maps of herbs
or stars that I would reach
locate what I do not know.
Going to a precipice made of rose
or ocher, bronze to give an area
of silence. To trace forward into chance.
Daffodils beginning to sleeve.

The equinox in six days.
How each line finds what matters
subject to horizontal light, stained glass
where I'd sliver bits of seeing.

Each instant of focus
facets different degrees.
Where voices echo toward a curving tree.
Appetite furthers hunger.

Argus, the god of peripheries,
rods and cones catching it
out of corners. When verbs perform
actions, pen scorches lightning
roughs up textures. When extension occurs

pen glides the third month sky.
I retrieve my name among penstamons

or recover balance on the elm stump.
Still the equinox four days off.

quote:
Philip Whalen—
Scenes of Life at the Capital

Motion, Pattern, Aroma

How sets free time in gardening.

In light waves, a plume occurs.

To cite crows fence back owl slips

Mid-sentence clears psychic
curved space.

Not connecting on the phone
I send a letter across town.

All morning following scales through
the bare elm.

So what times I discover
crowns the leaves' reticulations

And proves what's random.

Frees gardening in how time sets me
in motion, pattern, aroma.

When I talk stages, blanks,
tables, spirals.

Cite what tries to hide.

Asleep in my lap at the reading
your eyelids' netted veins.

Vigas overhead, mindrift parting, the weight
in my arms.

Between solidity and what alters, elm seeds
stuck in a shoe.

What resembles the sky
where rain evaporates before it hits?

Wings sound the air

Plane just above.

To recover what selves
exist in composition.

A bed of volunteers: bachelor buttons,
larkspur, ox-eye daisies.

Trying on clothes of persuasion:
sign, compost, destiny, articulation.

Of what lives the planet can hold
which places sustainable.

Splotches of water where pruned grapevines bleed.

Chaco and Back

All dwellings constructed in
solar direction.

Dust rows, buttes to tell how much energy remains.

Bus run shakes the hand, the boys
asleep two seats in front.

Casa Rinconada quartz-eye conclusions
300 years span the eye.

Ink camera word plan
the place in snow imagined.

This heavy wall stems three stories
in the shadow of a talus slope.

How to reach what's desired
bus on a dirt road.

What's mine before the view, the Alto Mesa Trail overlooks.

The halogen light adjusted to its peak
glows around the page.

Some chrysanthemums & carnations still alive.

Hold thermometer to range climate
this symposium of rays.

Where to go when flow is interrupted?

Tin chimes reflect silver light
on your cheeks and forehead.

It's morning comes through
the streaked windshield.

Then to orient within larger ruins.

Keep in mind just how autumn prolongs itself.

Chaco road, mold masonry
tops placed to stabilize walls.

Looking for lizards in the Great Kiva, thin air alone.

Rock park makeshift puddle, to want it all.

Let's alter how long inside light
adjacent windows sight travels.

Sliver moon blinks the evaporating sky.

Core & veneer masonry, brown hues, sometimes white.
Crow wing glints green in fierce light.

Sun Dagger, ray-splice, tree ring dating
where vigas remain.

Bladder press full force stops the bus.
Lettuce seeds scatter the breeze.

On Enchanted Mesa the crow caw marvels.

What's spent now leaves dry, placing them down
the bodies embedded in so many walls.

The Ojito

for Ken Tabbish

a fire sharpens in the pulse of gypsum
    to mark the day
        brown gloves on talus rock
    in the swell of rifts
        the Ojito
      sulfur cliffs
      salt lingers
    to escape the wind
dry blue ink on thumb nail
      to compass a rock bridge
    how time focuses
      agave conducts wind
turns an angry sun aside
    nib catches a ray
      not just potential
    links in the actual
      reach for light
        on the year's shortest day
        cold hands
        remember summer's heat
near mineral springs
    a precise geodesy
      fire
wry in a foreign tongue
      bound so near
        the foot's next step

eludes the silt
is in the ink's shadow
circling

Ink Pattern

He cannot myth the witness
echoes of the slight.
What suffices
as weight character
is dismissed
in a supper of margins.

That
he stars in absence
is a not belonging to
the door
entered.

The structure of dirt
under his fingernails
is elusive
if only an inquiry
a crystal survey
might be
filtered.

***

The reach of her spine
multiplies the ground
each step sticks
to sure feet.

Geological voyages
snap a view
command vigilence
retreat from
final sufficiency.

O news   old lines
determine the ink patterns'
drift:
consonance apart.

***

She recalls a scant
wire of success
a harsher
meaner land.

The indignant integers queue.

The room is
redolent of synthesizers
the pulse in tomorrow's paralysis.
The air
power through her lungs
is not the verb
of disaffection

the x-ray
heat projected from her
an equation of pressure
curled in voice

her thrust
concaving broader arcs.

She describes the breadth
of fugues
the reproduction
of polygons
her longing
to divide.

**

The morning star is
but a deranged pupil
of the sun.

In the east
much north.

The magnets repel
latitudinal drift.

She propels
what he gesticulates:
somersaulting procedures.

Not a monument
a desire to translate the language
at once.

They.   Weight
the toll.

In Position

Alongside the house, proportion alters.

Toward sky past noon reach, what's a world for?

To begin the run, motion's needed, or to get out the door.

To touch the wall bears a spark.

Whatever's a passion, energy retrieves.

Tender the right condition, the planet's tilt.

A child's voice, barely audible, the traffic's drone.

What will freeze this evening?

And then purple reaches the eye, and morning becomes
selective.

A bit of chocolate lingers, walnut texture, chewy lines.

Olive oil on the paper, cloud sun closing.

Just the climatic balm for sun-wary travelers.

Marigold's neon in the afternoon light.

Cactus amber dahlias, spikey datura seed pods.

What's the aroma after it's cut?
Soon time to trade seeds, transitional performance.

Where it's not about, but in position, proposition.

When jet time marvels, a fear shade angles.

Basil, upended, holds the night aroma.

To step on the flagstone, the wind seed skeletons,
next in line.

Allows Sketches

Weeds push through asphalt.
Gray demeanor, vacant basketball court.
The cirrus sky, a rotting tree.

A roof corrugates desire
to be elsewhere.

Still lines follow
quickening eyes
describe sanguine signs.

What intervals are
in this fiction?
To gather leaves
dapple asphalt's crooked

seams, the hand knots

what it wants.
Astride the fence
ailanthus sprouts

anywhere seeds fall.
Horizontal, most glances
go unread. Darting out

the side, a grasshopper
fiddles the reedwind.

What figures allude?

The backboard's shadow
a sundial's reprieve.
At noon all movement's possible.

A taste of corn
angles the remembrance.
A boy on the playground

dribbles into sketches.
Loose geometry of bankshots.
Hours accrete tenuously.

Whether variable or fixed
unaccountably the place triggers

recognition across the acts.

Obsidian

Where it's dislocated from the original place at least twice,
it has an energy charge that is conducive to

Or reaches you at some sense beyond what you think
you came for.

Can suggest or pronounce states of energy that you can't.

Whether they are rich or not, how you give attention
to the family of veins.

To lead on, direct, cause to form, or upend the structure
itself.

Or be changed in orientation.

The obsidian's black mirror attracts sun, cools the eye.

To set margins differently is not always easy.

It catches the gaze, throws back depth glass shine.

And then carpets, keyboards, fly the music room.

Wants to put no marks on the bare wall, but the page
is waiting for its blackness to extend.

Directs what reaches optical nerve endings touch in
light's memoranda.

Wine's velocity locates the winged manic station.

The only arrowhead I've turned up back garden to
cultivate sharpness.

Tunes color to claim on re:verse angles of approach.

Clouds morning section, long time flees the scope,
glass not native to back garden soil, tomatoes.

If it is quickness alone, water seeps slowly in humus.

What holds cloudburst lightning drought tolerant reading?

That tends plot scene action, not according to ease
but planting.

Star Garden

Scorpio breaks the night—
we can't see the garden
leaves signify presence—

a rock steeps
the moon's pinwheel.

Each breath re-
volves conspiracies
crooked lines

of sage, jay screech
memory's pan-

demonium.

The Big Dipper splits
juniper scent engages

the skylight's
notes. You in-

volve a weed
blade to open

yet another glyph.

Not Masterpieces,
Planting Astonishments
for Karen

No matter how long
you work it

letters are scrawls, turnabouts,
astonishments, strokes, cuts, masks.

Transplant sedum in clefts
of a stone walk. Place

bunch onions. Light plays, hair
askew. Not enough heat to germinate

kale seeds. Another chance
to stroke moss, trace

filaments. Correspond the plot
we cultivate to a place

unmade in provisional stance,
a crazy row that includes, not

final sounds, resounds
the columbine shoots. Against

the trellis, grapes
Spanish broom. Keep script

in mind, rehearse
the aging compost.

Cloud bellies tornado blue
on the near horizon.

A chill rivers me.
My body's curves, a sufficiency

that ages. Not masterpieces
digging, planting astonishments.

Who knows climatic waves?
Hands in the humus build

this bed the climate forms.
Its charms present your body

fatigue's pleasure
a desiring escape.

What scrawls gravel
slips the words into day

frames our affection
to a wily degree.

To extend syllables & retreat
cuts boundaries, each blade

& night turnabout
the larkspur, a jagged

volunteer to disperse
pollen, spore desire

burn the alphabet's buoyant mask.

quote:
Susan Howe—
"These Flaws and Generosities of the Heart:
  Emily Dickinson and the Illogic of Sumptuary Vales"

Residence in the High Desert

1

Primrose can take the whole
bed's desert over.

Toward a variety of possible sage.

Is it dahlias or canna lilies
bloom longest?

When dirt's between toes and
sandals stick to the feet.

Tend an agency of action
to ground and circulate.

A currency of light speculation

Finds lightning on the high mesa.

Around a visual alphabet.

The neuron's myelin
against electrical swarms.

A child opens an umbrella.
Veins against the cloud.

Rays on the table.
Later than I intended to stay up.

Unplugged the neighbor's electric
bug zapper

To pass over silence.

Then the fireworks from
our roof.

Sustained finale:
the grandest flash suffices the retinal desire.

Moon: trapped in elm branches
steady among these flashes.

Now is the time to attend.

Even drowsiness allures.

As passions splay out the
game that would contain them.

A chaos of night cicadas
indicates summer heat.

Time torn reasoning, specificity
unmasks the vague, not the oblique.

2 AM: I wish the Spanish broom

were still ascent.
Desert can overtake the whole
bed's primrose.

Not long enough to be called a drought.

The broadsides not yet on the wall.

Creates its own momentum
in the cognitive sonar.

To locate points of flexibility
in the spine.

Play the desire to spiral.

Feta, olives, eggplant in garlic, basil.

Turn gladness to the parapet.

He in whom joy ascends.
Comprehension based on breadth.

To overtake the whole primrose bed
the desert flees

A dense scrutiny.

Capers, stuffed grape leaves, artichoke hearts.

How a new residence roots

filaments of light.
A summer sky lofts into cumulus.

Datura spreads without cultivation
but dahlias crave intensive care.

Never too many Roma tomatoes.

To engage a leafy plot
is no completion in itself.

2

Three bees feeding in the datura
just popped open

Waiting to see what color the hibiscus blooms.

Disks of burgundy against light
green, rolling, hovering.

Bataglia, caponata, focaccia.

Lilliput zinnias in front of the bed.

Where, if I work over,
a certain charge builds.

A stunned glance at the rays
a morning glory.

At night the orange tabby's a fleeting blur.

Three datura feeding on just bees
popped open.

They last about 17 hours

Before wilt sets in.

Twice in one week, praying mantises
devouring bees among datura.

Dead head the wilted blossoms first season ever.

Woke with a car alarm scraping my ears.

Still alive, the futile struggle to get out.

Georgia O'Keeffe opens datura to a long gaze.

Trouble getting back to sleep.

Where fools eat the seeds & flowers
hoping for a wild ride.

Turn the bell riverwards
for sky response.

Pollen thick on their legs.

In this light

How they become invisible.

Gutter pools, an oily sky.

Corn meal & sage in each room.

A child recalls showers
say parasols vein the rain

Below seasonal moisture.

Black roasted coffee, scones, cream,
blueberries.

The reachable and what eludes.

Just popped open the feeding datura
three bees.

At the beginning of a great career
felling a blighted elm.

Strained light, dazzlements through
blond oak sashes.

The filaments, a family adheres
or cuts apart.

Replace light bulb front porch.

Stave off the prickly seed pods.

A cottonwood boar alights on the ficus.

Cognitive rivulets course
the backyard: collide, collaborate.

A sharp-shinned hawk, or a falcon
screeches spotted wings.

Affect lodges early morning's undiluted scents.

3

The cosmos flower bleeds burgundy
into light.

Dryest July in years
August, now September, torrential.

Calavacitas, maiz, chile.

Line torque multiplies possibilities.

The family scrambles from the car.

Droplets on the dahlia

Poised, at touch they petal into
a small puddle.

As if on the far edge of the roof
a thundering.

Climb lightning tone scintillates
the tune.

The flower's light bleeds cosmos
into burgundy.

Afterwards the letters soak into the ground.
How rain records its alphabet.

As tone conduit for new scents

Roasted chile burns memory of fall.

Possibility plies multi-line torque.

A hummer in autumn sage.

Perennials plant their own discretion
sculpt singularity in their bed.

Air charges morning scent
electric in the olfactory.

Bagels, pecans, oranges, apple juice, espresso.

3 AM: din of distant cars passes over
the arrival of sleep.

Collocate lines of zinnias
bloom mazy.

The canale drains into the bell peppers.

Builders of these flat roofs
when the leaks come through.

Delphinium as amulet
blues the retinal shade.

The family soaked from driveway to front door.

Diverse signals relinquish
a composite into place.

Learn angles, U-turn round
find cholla hops into the leg.

A lunar cinema last night of August.

The canna torches up to.

Wet petals on the table, chianti, olives, bread.

Lash silence to a divergent sky.

4

Birds comma the slight wind.

Sudden afternoon shades
a blue spruce chill.

Intention shuffles the wits.

Mushrooms kiss the rotted trees.

Diverse motion in the light above town.

Wild columbine, chanterelles, bluebells, aspens.

Needles descend a dead fir, spinrays.

Elevation bends perspective, scents
sound, wetter, cooler

Gives sight a hand, currency a ground.

Coexistence of the varied seams.

Winds bird the slight comma

Heat the enigmas, rising to
Sweatshirt sticking, the pen pressed moist.

Punctuation flies the cadence
to a plot composed breeze.

As if each puddle contains a pond
swims the skin.

Moisture bounds kind limits of dryness.

Rosemary, oregano, garlic, pineapple sage.

What the extended hand passes in
labor extends

Elusive figures in lateral scope.

Commas slight the wind birds.

If piñon pines etch the hills
starkness ambers autumnal mapping.

5 AM: I can't go back to sleep.

Stillness, an intense act.

Watering in dark morning contours
the columbine poised

To receive air, time sensing
a pause in the petals' quick release.

5

Zinnias tangle through the canna lilies
competing for light.

Hummingbirds find pineapple sage.

Chamisa, amber clouds, tufting the ground.

What flies up, what settles
the near horizon hazes.

Intoxicates the beat of wings
exhausts the body, or just the eye?

Difficult season for allergies.

Lofts skyward as we drive the river north.

Permission to arrange this place down
where the breath pushes out.

Will sculpts a provisional arroyo

Sun anvils surprise in midday heat.

Composure stretches across stares in class.

Light lilies through the zinnia tangles
competing for cannas.

Permitted to return to a pro-
position that home shifts provisions.

Grapes, tea, brandy, cookies.

As if it were a book modulating its feasts.

Learning to stand on one leg extended.

The body's geometric promise
relates context or contiguity.

A chasm across cultures.

Consider duration of jet noise
the season of crysanthemums.

Repose refracts lightly.

North on Carlisle, the glare catches
pupils wide open.

The interstate rolls up, curious the chamisa
still blooming in higher elevations.

Than here, where else the complex matters so much?
Red chile, rice, enchiladas, beans, dark beer.

2 PM again. The sand, skeletal cholla
bitten off sharply.

Over the city, ambient noise ubiquitous.

A double skylight glares, subdivides plots
but rock piles its own patterns northeastward.

Than there, where sounds a marching band in practice.

Research to be done in wood.

Inclined to activate the view of objects.

Subject to the veins in rock.

Rearrangments of residential treatment policies.

Taking the poem to play in the construct of homes.

Chimes sound distant
amid constant sprinklers.

Sun still hot enough to turn the face

Where motions cleanse, light bends
in autumn's ripe prism.

6

Chisel-nib bone flexible paints.

Dead canna foliage clearing the air.

Skeletal December, cherry tree not yet
one year in the ground.

Sunflower stalks still rooted

How fence shadows lengthen.

Bare light changes protection
self-caught nutrients.

Means to absorb and not be absorbed
exactly.

Smoke escapes the burner's door.

The way play reaches your tiny hands.

Pecans still cling to the tree.

Breaking twigs off the dried cosmos.

Makes the cold brittle scent of smoke.

Turn line cinders, ash flakes out the chimney.

When the hand turns cold indoors
do I want a fire?

Flexible bone chisels nib-paint.

Marigolds not yet picked cartwheel
the backside bed.

Where acts move in the viscera
power claims its due.

Night spreads itself over-roof.

Venus can't be seen through the skylight.

It bites hands chopping felled elm wood.

Shear insurance junk mail without opening.

Bare grapevines renew sight
angling past severe gestures.

Slightest blue remaining on the salvia.

Electrical meter turns sun on it
shadow cast back.

Phone line out nine days two months in a row.

Running down Inspiration Dr. SE past
whatever details of

To move pallid light.

Top leaves of the photinia turn rust.

Escalates desire to listen.

Leaves lower to the ground persist
in bright green.

Hundreds of tiny larkspur.

Poorly written rhyme's easy to deflect.

Garlic chive stems seedless.

Praise notes' ephemera, cool down
the piano range.

Years ahead of everyone else.

Third season of your life
to think of you retrieving me back here.

As if a canna were figuring its own death.

The distance of apricots blossoming.

Try sign language this gray afternoon.

Along lines of exercise, I follow dahlia bones.

How we read glee in each others' irises.

4 AM: the sound of wrestling from the cradle.

A pot of Italian roast

I tunnel the earliest morning hues
with pen and razor knife.

To locate the intersection of possible and actual

Where tips of light urge the gray.

7
for Ken Tabish

Agave spines shadow the page.

Follow in ambling gait
tossed dry gladness.

Jet roar abandons the pinon pine.

Soughing, strewing, broadcasting

About early noon winter solstice eve.

Rocks provide windbreak solar heat.

Awake at 1 AM to get hot milk.

Chamisa roots like rope
wind down the dry river bed.

As more vision is in sight.

Where granite's smooth.

You show me the owl clutching
a trout 20 yards downstream, ascending.

Shadows page the spine's agave.

Speculation provokes many days.

Waist deep in grasses to stride
alluvial plane.

The escarpment West: Mt. Taylor drifts
dizzy the horizon.

Footprints trace deer tracks, cholla.

How sand fans out before the gaze.

Whereas I'd enjoy jumping out of my skin
I take a drink of icy water.

We have time for late afternoon azure
loose sand.

Motion lights gratitude for a lone copper rock.

Sun sneeze, stamping feet.

Hack cough teases unseasonable warmth.

West out the Sandias for coffee, B & B.

Just enough wind to willow out.

The way that owl became your totem

Safe enough to regard.

Pages spine the agave shadow
still rays move cleanly.

Timing and action don't always coincide.

To close eyes and follow red floaters
under eyelids.

Bare light breath figures, the remainder silence.

8

for Mary Rising Higgins

Ice crystals pattern the windshield
mornings to scrape them, clear the view.

Wake to snow light reflecting 5 AM:
auditors in a dizzy referendum.

New muddy tires that grip.

No bird tracks in the bright yard.

Apple seedling's top leaves cling to twig branch.

Penstemon's fading green powder, dry membranes.

Sandias cloaked, my feet wet
melt rills to the Rio Grande.

Spotty moon, striated dusk.

How ambient noise muffles
the city's halt.

Red valerian bowed in the snow.

We walk your first storm.

Day shadows the lengthening fence post.

To possess the mine of winter.
Forecast for tomorrow, widely scoured shatters.

Today tone of browngray, this
to make still.

The listener shifts density or destiny.

The window catches sudden rays
more stands the wood.

Amoxicillin fluid curls tips of your hair.

Toward the quaquaversal, hot range options.

Avails dead tomato vines, turn
line, not sequence, motion curls.

A day for deep watering
dry ground, sky cast over.

Butt cold on a plastic chair.

Where is the terminus of varied attentions?

How many the hands, the lips
you express in random screeches.

Physicality of clammy feet
you hold up my hands.

The practice of observing outside.

Crystals ice the wind, shield
the view, clear morning, scrape.

Not fictions, word valences that extend
Bare dead hibiscus branches.

What's needed pushes the ground
channels develop, the auditor's poised.

The cat crouches alert mouse hunting.
Air shivers the nose, still you sleep.

Second brief snow down, three days later clear sky heat.

Bird singing over car rumble
where connectives generate, satisfaction finds a base.

Xeriscaping, not zeroscaping.
January's last day midway through the decade.

Try to compose early as a book of hours
rearranging night and morning.

Seven nights without a fire.

To uproot dead sunflower stocks.

7:15 AM: no frost to scrape

To open still the flux, particular rays
more restless than any noon shadow.

9

Fluency in change is a book
that tosses hours about.

In morning, light snow on the berm.

San Mateo & Zuni, heavy traffic.

The conversation of rain and birds
sound texture release.

6 AM: I stand on one leg and listen:

Course times water is an integral sinking.

How to undermine the local routine.

Covered the peach tree three nights
against late winter frost.

When moments are surrounded by
unpredicted movement

Sight passes impasse.

As context meets cortex
funnel clouds against the bright sky.

Blooms set lunar night freezing
aphids devour last year's kale.

Not the thing itself, speculation on the thing.

Arms stretched out, you take in all in wavering gaze.

Strands the daylight, clears the view.

Write around the clock
linked sight wishes an accomplice.

To crack a jump in perception.

Steady plot, overhead elm seeds green
bushels to germinate, be weeded.

Chick Corea's "Spain," cabernet, baklava, French roast.

Not place alone determines relations
spacial tendencies.

Optimal light two days prior to the equinox.

About change a book of fluency
lines hours and tosses.

11:30 PM: the cats outside, you sleep.

Should not stay the night wake longer
but a short walk outside, the stars blurred.

Lilacs still tight budded.

Aphids on broccoli, columbine, daisies
tenderest portions.

Practice walking the house silently
so that power's in lightness.

To stretch one centimeter longer.

Already apricots the size of little finger tips.

To survive cold wind, to look after ripening.

You persist in banging on the radio.

To travel the capillaries' far current
the cherry tree's first blossom ever.

Suddenly to follow scents not yet present.

We play on the floor during the reading.

The port's trickle on tongue and gums.

10:45 PM: two days after the equinox
a restless wind purls.

Anticipates Spanish broom, red valerians,
needed rest.

7:30 AM in a cold metal room to teach.

Tumbleweeds blow with traffic north on I-25
into little bits rushing on the shoulder.

Never unusual wind spring tours the storm
bright moisture.

The sound from San Mateo & Zuni fiercer.

Remove back chimes to ensure right sleeping.

10

Grass silver in early morning light.

10 PM: the sky a milky haze, looks like snow.

An outsider, the breath fogs.

As satellite to the planet warns light
ranges direction.

The apricots burning in spring freeze.

South to mesquite, big horn sheep petroglyphs.

Grit wind bites the face to turn back.

Which square foot entices scrutiny
magnifies the scope of residence?

Grape leaves on a redwood post
pass circumference of what's said.

Means to breathe as to reside.

South through Corona, Ancho, Carrizozo.

As seldom seen smoke
an herb garden in perpetual array.

The strength of fresh orange juice, toast,
blueberry preserves.

April 10, the latest snow in eleven years.

Bike riding when the wind calms.
Series interrupts sequence at its own discretion.

Russian sage to attract hummers.

Slept with window open, first time since October.

To root out premature conclusions.

The rudeness of an alarm that persists through the
wee hours.

Olive trees, cottonwoods define spring winds.

You sleep in the car southeast of the Manzanos.

Silver mornings in light grass early.

When the snake petroglyph performs energy
along the eye's dance.

A flurry at peripheral vision
blows to the fore.

Never in the same arroyo twice.

The waiter's counter drumming awakes you.

Have them at your attention to drop the spoon.

Gypsum dried white sand where the ground has shaken.

The road map tears down several seams.

Erases towns, cancels subdivisions.

Droplets on the end of vigas
shade brings freely.

A pillow over the head doesn't muffle the alarm.

Open the window, delicious cool air
suffuses a lack of sleep.

Light angles dawn incision
to converse with birds & coffee.

The frigerator handle focuses a ray's fleeting brilliance.

Joshua Redman's where power claims equal shares.

Three adults couldn't prevent you from
breaking the Hoffman bowl.

Where ability and intensity coincide.

Crisp bright final day of April
stirs desire into a future that eludes.

11

Tern darts the air's molecular maze.

A block north of Barcelona Road to buy peppers.

The lace light patterns, the fray's cloudy sky.

Comprehension in broad sweeps
desires its own calculus.

Which admits a tern's parabola.

Who'd sleeve my arms in cool air?

6:30 AM: bare feet on concrete.

Across a breadth of contacts
the world fires.

In the vicinity, at least, tactile, promising.

10 PM: in 28 hours, 35 minutes, you turn one.

On my lap looking up: oscillating fan blades in your pupils.

Late night spreads its electric familiar across the sky.

To spend cause just approval
the reward in chiles, pimentos, tomatillos.

Morning stripes moist across the gaze.

A painter of space, could you alone have brushed this?

Violet larkspur through the French door.

Grapevines to be trained upward.

To mine this mesa west of Blake, south of Sage.

Electronic dumping ground
when the city grows.

The shade of two juniper trees contiguous.

The lawnmower-car kicks up dust, noise.

What dumping on the mesa reflects
about its subjects.

Air's dart mazes the molecular tern.

To find virtue residing in the diverse.

What particularity can be generalized?

The stump that serves as a chopping block
in the midst of bachelor buttons, larkspur.

The slightest brush where we're in thrall to Eros night
book enables language, the plum.

Tendrils of the grapevine quick to apprehend the fact.

Not to rave, to reside pulse, size sculpting channels, arroyos.

Glimpses the lines of your body contiguous in delight.

You're persistent to respond
if on the other side, desire's arc.

Listen through magnetism to be seized
in an instant, a hummingbird sings tunnels, towers.

Calendula both orange and amber.

How the two swerve into, vie for sky's territory.

Cycle south on Washington Avenue over I-40 into the wind.

A lawn of bindweed flowers.

Molecules tern the dart maze air:
root sky flares, memory lodges.

To sustain the visceral's province
time eager edge, the train.

With compass found sculpture
the mesa's junk electronic familiar.

12
for John Brandi

Unwilling plane rackets the air's membrane.

Dried husk of cicada hangs on the clothesline.

Synoptic view of the yard's partial in spite of comprehension.

Pull up the ninth tomato plant sucked dry
by curly leaf virus.

Century plant's long slow effulgence
death, offspring from the roots.

Energy moves in each direction
but form's in sitting down long enough.

Empty places startle the garden
but this year pole beans climb.

"This is my fifteenth cup of coffee today"
raises the waiter's eyebrows, one table over.

How to redirect attention when you insist on breaking boundaries.
4 PM: pick snails out from under garlic chives.

To interpret experience is not separate from reading.

Naked skin too warm in summer air.

Curly leaf virus attacks when we're in CA.

This notes a poetry reading in between the reader.

Set a drip system to save water.

The light's property blurs Falling Man.
Where sunflowers look backward world in.

In the morning rainwater in flip flops, a twig.

Nasturtiums, bursts of orange dotting the bed.
Comb lightning, stare rain seeping.

Racket wills, unairs the membrane.

More caffeine than anyone needs.

Fettucine, red peppers, garlic, pinot grigio.

White hibiscus, scarlet inner ring alters the gaze.

Plant zucchini and butternut in late June to elude squash bugs.
2 AM: steps on the snail while peeing.

Laid paper texture roughens the ink
round stic medium.

Clumps of Interlocken white grapes, partial light,
haze pendulous, not yet sweet.

Elevate to Sandias to escape July's heat.

Penstamon, yarrow, aspen, fir
grasshoppers rasp the air.

Check view valley, the Rio Grande winds across
a rock hammers below.

Datura lambent in the night, crickets surprise the cicadas.

Snail squashes under ball of the foot
oozes through toes.

Where hands are deciduous the proper study's
to sketch around the boy moves plants, animals.

And red glenora grapes sweet, to do a dervish swirl

Available when taste waits.

Late afternoon shade, back against a warm wall
grapes and merlot on tongue.

Ten days later, we beg for moisture
an ant traverses the window sash.

Membrane unplanes the will's racket air.

Sweat twists the sheets.

Reprieve, release, withholding discrete bits
fan blades oscillate, the season sticks.

Colophon

Set in *ITC Berkeley Old Style*,
a typeface based on Frederic W. Goudy's
original design for the University of California
in 1938 and released by Lanston Monotype in 1956
as *Californian*. Tony Stan redrew it in 1983
for a furthered life. As with other Goudy faces,
joyous idiosyncracies enliven—ascenders higher
than capitals, curved arm of "k" and
his beloved *old guys* "e".

•

Book design by J. Bryan

John Tritica studied at the University of California, San Diego, Lund University in Sweden, and Miami University, which culminated in a Ph.D. from the University of New Mexico and a dissertation on Kenneth Rexroth. While in Sweden, he met the poet Niklas Törnlund whose work he translated— *All Things Measure Time* (published by The Landlocked Press.) Tritica's reviews, essays, and poems have been published extensively in literary magazines for years. He lives with his family in Albuquerque, where he teaches gifted students at Albuquerque High School.